EXT... ...5

WORLD'S
BIGGEST
DINOSAURS

Rupert Matthews

Raintree

www.raintreepublishers.co.uk
Visit our website to find out more information about Raintree books.

To order:
☎ Phone 0845 6044371
🗎 Fax +44 (0) 1865 312263
🖳 Email myorders@raintreepublishers.co.uk

Customers from outside the UK please telephone +44 1865 312262

Raintree is an imprint of **Capstone Global Library Limited**, a company incorporated in England and Wales having its registered office at 7 Pilgrim Street, London, EC4V 6LB – Registered company number: 6695582

Text © Capstone Global Library Limited 2012
First published in hardback in 2012
First published in paperback in 2013
The moral rights of the proprietor have been asserted.

Edited by Rebecca Rissman and Laura Knowles
Designed by Richard Parker
Picture research by Mica Brancic
Originated by Capstone Global Library Ltd
Printed and bound in China by CTPS

ISBN 978 1 406 23461 9 (hardback)
15 14 13 12 11
10 9 8 7 6 5 4 3 2 1

ISBN 978 1 406 23468 8 (paperback)
16 15 14 13 12
10 9 8 7 6 5 4 3 2 1

British Library Cataloguing in Publication Data
Matthews, Rupert.
World's biggest dinosaurs. -- (Extreme dinosaurs)
567.9-dc22
A full catalogue record for this book is available from the British Library.

Acknowledgements
We would like to thank the following for permission to reproduce images: © Capstone Publishers pp. **4** (James Field), **5** (Steve Weston), **6** (Steve Weston), **7** (James Field), **8** (James Field), **9** (Steve Weston), **10** (James Field), **11** (Steve Weston), **13** (James Field), **14** (Steve Weston), **15** (James Field), **16** (James Field), **17** (Steve Weston), **20** (James Field), **21** (Steve Weston), **22** (James Field), **23** (James Field), **24** (Steve Weston), **25** (James Field), **26** (Steve Weston), **27** (James Field); © Miles Kelly Publishing p. **19** (Rudi Vizi); Shutterstock p. **29** (© Mark R Higgins).

Background design features reproduced with permission of Shutterstock/© Szefei/© Fedorov Oleksiy/© Oleg Golovnev/© Nuttakit.

Cover image of a *Paralititan* reproduced with permission of © Capstone Publishers/James Field.

We would like to thank Nathan Smith for his invaluable help in the preparation of this book.

Every effort has been made to contact copyright holders of material reproduced in this book. Any omissions will be rectified in subsequent printings if notice is given to the publishers.

Contents

Some words are shown in bold, **like this**.
You can find out what they mean by
looking in the glossary.

World of giants

The **dinosaurs** were a group of animals that lived millions of years ago. Some dinosaurs were the biggest animals that ever walked on Earth. *Apatosaurus* was 23 metres long, about twice as long as a bus. The hunter *Saurophaganax* was 11 metres long, more than twice as long as a car.

Saurophaganax

Apatosaurus

Did you know?

Torosaurus had the largest head of any land animal. It was 2.4 metres long. That's longer than an average bed!

Torosaurus

African monster

Sauropods were huge plant-eaters with very long necks and tails. One type of sauropod was called *Paralititan*. It was over 26 metres long and weighed about 63 tonnes. A single bone from its front leg was as long as an adult human is tall. Scientists found **fossils** of *Paralititan* in rocks that used to be part of a coastline. They think it may have swum between islands.

Paralititan

Did you know?
Paralititan was the
largest **dinosaur** to
live in Africa.

The long neck

One of the longest **dinosaurs** was a **sauropod** called *Diplodocus*. It grew to be 27 metres long. That is longer than the length of a swimming pool. Sauropods lived in herds. The younger animals walked in the centre where they could be protected by the larger, older dinosaurs.

Diplodocus

Did you know?

Some sauropods, such as *Saltasaurus*, had bone **armour** on their backs to protect them from attack.

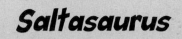

Saltasaurus

Earth shaker

Imagine a **dinosaur** so big it made the ground shake when it walked. That was *Seismosaurus*. Its name means "Earthquake Lizard". The **fossil** skeleton was so big it took scientists 13 years to **excavate** all of it.

Did you know?

Seismosaurus may have been able to make a deafening noise by cracking its tail like a whip.

Horned face

Ceratopsian dinosaurs were plant-eaters with horns on their heads. *Triceratops* was the largest of the ceratopsians. It grew to be 9 metres long and weighed about 4 tonnes. That is as heavy as an elephant. The three horns on its head were nearly one metre long and very sharp. They may have been used to fight off attacks by hunters, such as the *Tyrannosaurus*, shown here.

Triceratops

Old toothy

Shantungosaurus spent most of its life on all fours but it could also walk on just its back legs. It was 15 metres long and may have weighed over 14.5 tonnes. That is heavier than three Asian elephants. This makes it the largest animal ever to walk on two legs.

Shantungosaurus

Did you know?
Shantungosaurus
had 2,500 teeth in
its massive jaws.

Pack hunter

Dromaeosaurs were hunting **dinosaurs** with large claws on their back legs. *Utahraptor* weighed nearly half a tonne. It grew to be 7 metres long, about the same as two dolphins. It may have hunted in packs in order to bring down animals larger than itself. *Utahraptor* was the largest of the dromaeosaurs.

Utahraptor

Did you know?
The huge claw on *Utahraptor's* back foot was used to kill prey.

Giant glider

Pterosaurs were flying **reptiles** that had wings of leathery skin. The biggest pterosaur was *Quetzalcoatlus*, which lived in North America about 70 million years ago. It had a wingspan of about 14.5 metres, making it as big as a small aircraft. Many pterosaurs were quite small. They had a wingspan of only about 30 centimetres, the length of a ruler.

Great bites

Allosaurus was the biggest hunter of its day. It reached about 10 metres in length, nearly as long as a bus. *Allosaurus* had sharp 5-centimetre-long teeth that were V-shaped like a saw. The jaws of *Allosaurus* were hinged so that it could gulp down huge lumps of meat.

Allosaurus rests after a big meal

Did you know?

After a large meal *Allosaurus* may not have needed to eat again for more than a week.

Best crest

Hadrosaurs were four-legged plant-eaters who walked on two legs. They often had crests on their heads. The crest was made of hollow bones connected to the nose and may have been used to make loud sounds. *Parasaurolophus* had the biggest crest at about 1.5 metres long, nearly the height of an adult woman.

crest

Did you know?

Some scientists think that the head crest may have been used to push tree branches aside as *Parasaurolophus* walked through forests. But nobody really knows for sure.

The great hunter

Giganotosaurus was the biggest hunter on Earth. It was 13 metres long and weighed nearly 12 tonnes, so it was about as heavy as 60 lions. The skull of *Giganotosaurus* was the biggest of any meat-eating **dinosaur**. It was over 1.5 metres long.

Did you know?

Giganotosaurus may have lived
in family groups. They probably
quarrelled violently over a kill.

Living tank

Ankylosaurus was the largest of the **ankylosaurians**, or **armoured dinosaurs**. It was over 9 metres long, 1.5 metres wide, and weighed about 5.5 tonnes. That is about as heavy as an elephant. The armour covered almost its entire body – even its eyelids were covered by a bony flap.

Did you know?

Ankylosaurus had a heavy bone club on the end of its tail, which would have been a useful weapon if a hunter attacked it.

club

armour

Studying fossils

There are many steps to studying **dinosaur fossils**. First, scientists take a photo of the fossil. Then the fossil bones and teeth are fitted together to form a complete skeleton. Often some bones are missing. The skeleton is then used to imagine what the animal looked like when it was alive. Finally the scientist writes a description of the fossils and **publishes** it for others to read.

Glossary

ankylosaurians family of armoured plant-eating dinosaurs that lived between 160 and 65 million years ago

armour outer shell or bone on some dinosaurs that protected their bodies

ceratopsians family of horned plant-eating dinosaurs that lived in North America and Asia towards the end of the age of dinosaurs

dinosaur group of animals that lived on land millions of years ago during the Mesozoic Era. The Mesozoic Era is part of Earth's history that is sometimes called the "Age of Dinosaurs". It is divided into three periods: Triassic, Jurassic, and Cretaceous.

dromaeosaurs family of hunting dinosaurs that were able to run very quickly and had large claws on their back legs

excavate dig something out of the ground

fossil part of a plant or animal that has been buried in rocks for millions of years

hadrosaur family of plant-eating dinosaurs. They are also known as duckbills because many of them had wide, flat mouths that looked like the bill of a duck.

pterosaurs group of flying reptiles that lived between 220 and 65 million years ago

publish print in a book, newspaper, journal, or magazine

reptiles cold-blooded animals such as lizards or crocodiles

sauropods family of plant-eating dinosaurs that had long necks and long tails. The largest dinosaurs of all were sauropods.

Find out more

Books

Dinosaur Encyclopedia, Caroline Bingham (Dorling Kindersley, 2009)
Dinosaurs, Stephanie Turnbull (Usborne, 2006)
First Encyclopedia of Dinosaurs and Prehistoric Life, Sam Taplin (Usborne, 2011)

Websites

www.dinosaurden.co.uk
Information about dinosaurs, as well as puzzles and games can be found on this site.

www.nhm.ac.uk/kids-only/dinosaurs
The Natural History Museum's website has lots of information about dinosaurs, including facts, quizzes, and games.

www.oum.ox.ac.uk/thezone/fossils/index.htm
Learn more about fossils and how they form on this website.

www.thedinosaurmuseum.com/html/dinosaur-facts.html
Find out more about dinosaurs on the Dinosaur Museum website.

Index